About the Book

If one has been fortunate enough to have lived in a small coastal Maine community, such as Deer Isle, one can easily understand the desire to make poetry, to paint and to respond creatively to its aesthetic and evocative qualities. Permission is given for wide-ranging expressions whether in idiosyncratic forms of conventions, or not. Her poetry expresses a mood, a memory or direct observation with a desire to share it with others. Many of the poems have been published in a small Maine newspaper where readers often reach out with expressions of their relevance and with their understanding. The author accepts responsibility for freedom from normal restraints of formal poetry and for the poetic license when a moment is needed.

From *Here* to *There*

A Poetic Journal From Early Maine Mornings

Dee Dee Moore

authorHOUSE®

AuthorHouse™
1663 Liberty Drive
Bloomington, IN 47403
www.authorhouse.com
Phone: 1-800-839-8640

Published by AuthorHouse   04/12/2012

ISBN: 978-1-4685-7659-7 (sc)

Dedication

To family and friends who have encouraged and indulged me in this late-life passion. Thank you one and all. In the words of my favorite poet, Mary Oliver, "Poetry isn't a profession, it's a way of life. It's an empty basket; you put your life into it and make something out of it". I write poetry as an observer of the life forces around me and to live life more fully.

Contents

Island Lure

What is this magnet grabbing my spirit
Pulling from across the bridge
Promising a paradise found?
What charges my pulse
And sends it racing
In wild anticipation?

What power of Nature
Exerts such pull
Awakening my sleeping senses?
And beckons to me again and again
Luring me across
With promises of rejuvenation.

Bridges—A Way Across

Whether old or new, over cities or streams
Bearing heavy loads or a trickle of traffic
Whether aerodynamic wonders or puddle hoppers
With trusses, suspensions, arches or beams
There's obstacles to overcome, stories to be told
Both before and after they provided a way across.

Whether elegantly simple or marvels of engineering
Successes or failures, and there have been some of each.
From Galloping Gertie to the Hoover Dam Bypass
To destinies dreamed of, or simple adventures
Each greets the elements with awesome resolve
To weather the wind, ice or fog, and accept their limitations.

With our occasional doubts and fears aside
Our thankfulness felt is seldom spoken
Of the many splendid vistas provided
And memories of earlier journey's taken
We know the advantages and joys that they bring
And accept all of their gifts with much gratitude.

Rhythms Of The Sea

The pounding surf
Churning jewels from the sea
Brings eager seekers
Of excitement and mystery
And many small treasures
To fill their collectors' cravings.

As the evening calm
Returns the sea to its' mysterious past
Millions of distant stars
Accompany the bobbing shrimpers
Who court her bounteous rhythms
For a quiet dawn and abundant rewards.

Winter Harbor Lights

From a view at the Inn on the Harbor

Gently aroused
By a droning sound
I arise to a sliver of a moon
And millions of twinkling stars.
Though darkness prevails
The harbor is nearly filled
With tiny red and green lights
Attending to necessary tasks
Before moving briskly out of view.
By dawn quiet prevails
And their day well underway
A day that seemed like night
And will finish at the end of daylight.

Island Gifts To An Early Riser

As spectacular, crisp night skies, filled with stars
Give way to pink-hewed silhouettes
Of mountain peaks and regal firs
Across the reach

The stage is set for the show's brightest star
And her brilliant appearance rises skyward
Accompanied by soft voices
From both land and sea.

As the volume swells and the skies begin to fill with light
Birds and boats appear to be dashing across ribbons of water
As if rushing for front row seat
For this breath-taking performance.

But I know that I, as an early riser
Will be presented with these wondrous gifts
Again and again, with only slight variation
And never tire of the delight.

Visions Of A Boat Yard Christmas

Sparkling jewels lap at the boat yard's edges
Taunting the joyless shrink-wrapped vessels.
How can you hide from all those summer pledges
Of joyful jaunts and water's soothing wrestles?

How can you sleep with such joy to behold
With my plea to reject those white overdresses
While wind's whispers abound with messages bold,
Slip away, enjoy winter's cold, luminous tresses!

But hark! Dusk brings signs of newfound Christmas spirits
Twinkling lights appear beneath a fresh dusting of snow
Newly hung wreaths begin a rhythmic sway—we hear it!
Sea music's exultation, suddenly beginning to flow!

Inside Looking Out

Confining, though yet so comforting
On an early chilly morn
Just as dawn appears and silence is broken
When a few small creatures dart about.
Even shadows take on movements
When a breath of a breeze exhales
Prom ising new adventures
As the opening light begins to warm the spirits
The sense of confinement starts to disappear
Another day is viewed with awe
From the inside, looking out.

Winter's Graces

Ice crystals flare
Under the sun's brilliant rays
Shedding tears of joy.

Tiny birds scurry
Through cold and icy winds
Grateful for the berries.

Buds peek forth
From the hothouse of fallen leaves
Thankful for the sun.

Snow and ice retreat
Making footsteps welcome
In winter's wonderland.

Sunlight warms my room
And my dampened spirit
Bringing a joyful noise.

A Few Frosty Mornings

A few frosty mornings have paid us a visit
Left blankets on the lawn
Ice crystals on the mailbox
And hints of nature's artwork
Sure to return again.

The pup relished the romp
On the crunchy grass
Chasing melting ice crystals
As he raced in patterns lost
And celebrated new beginnings.

The pumpkins in the fields smiled
Adorned with brand new caps
And Mother Nature glowed
With her achievements
In this prelude to winter's gifts.

Images of the few frosty mornings
Quickly disappeared
Leaving only the overture
To elements which are sure to follow
When she returns with the full symphony.

A Joyful Season

At dawn's first light
A light kiss of snow
Delights all lovers
Of Mother Naure's gifts.

Boughs are beginning to bend,
Small creatures are casting about,
The air sings with anticipation
Soon sleds and shovels will appear.

Post lights still dim reluctantly
While the snow cover cradles their rays
And this brief incubation is welcome
As an announcement of a joyful season!

Tulips In Winter

From bulbs to blossoms
        right before my eyes
Tulips in winter
        what joy and surprise!

Unbothered by the wind or snow
        each perfect blossom rises
To the delight of its beholder,
        pink-tipped petals of near perfection.

And then a ritual begins
        first wide awake, then retreating
As day light turns to night
        a metamorphosis just beginning.

Much to the surprise and delight
        of its beholder
A new form begins to appear
        totally different from the other.

And unlike its springtime counterparts
        subject to the woes of wind and rain
The winter tulips don new faces
        as if ready to begin again.

Now carpels and stamens take center stage
        as tulip petals curl below
With brand new costumes
        from whom would ever guess, a tulip.

And then, as if to leave a legacy
        behold, new growth below
A scene offering total delight
        new baby bulbs for a future show.

Snowshoe Tracks

Hanging there with so many stories
Are crumbling rawhide lacings on hardwood frames
Revealing tell-tale signs of years gone by,
And adventures across wind-blown fields
That made the heart flutter with anticipation.

Oh, there are those newer models
Of metal, plastic or synthetic invention.
But can they offer the magical advantures,
The promise of joy with each new trail
Or the stories recalled from my first showshoe adventures.

Spring Is Spring

Darting, dipping, diving, into a tiny noisy den
Where weeks of careful preparation, and miraculous oval deposits
Now finds clamoring beaks, awaiting their wiggly bounty.

And then the chirping stops, until another feast arrives
And cries of delight ensue, with claims quickly swallowed
Over and over, the same routine, seemingly without end.

Then nourishment appears less often, a quiet settles in
Days go by and still no signs of the noisy occupants
Though occasional swaying hints of launching preparations.

Finally, parental urging comes from a nearby branch
One tiny occupant squeezes out, fluffs it feathers, and takes the plunge.
A maiden flight to a nearby perch, and then as quickly comes another.

A survey of their new surrounds, a hop from branch to branch
Adroitly darting one after another, testing their new found skills
Readying for the next adventure, eager to be completely sprung!

Nature's Nursery

OH DEAR,

Is this heavy dew or frost
Upon these branches of life
Weighing down conclusions
Carrying potential strife?

BUT WAIT!

The sun warms this glistening chalice
Of nature's versant nectar
Offering the hope and expectations
Of a newborn's specter!

LOOK HERE!

Buds bursting forth
Faint colors lifting coyly
Awaking nature's cry
As newborns open joyfully.

Oh Deer!

Oh how I waited for those tight little buds
On sturdy stems with supporting casts
Swaying in the slightest breeze
As if in dress rehearsal
For the performance soon to follow.

And then you blithely came along
Sucked them from their stems
Oblivious to my anticipation
And, with resulting sense of deprivation
You brought the curtain down!

With Mother Nature's bounteous table
Why must your lips choose these delights
Was it simply random plundering
That let you snatch their budding beauty
And deprive me of the joy they promised?

The Garden's Message

Artemisia, bougainvillea, stars of Persia, lambs ears and goats beards
Elegant, simple and mysterious names standing as a cast of characters,
Each with a part to play in this tapestry's warp and weft of life.

None demanding more attention than the other
Perennially accepting their role in this season of plentitude
Accepting as well, their places in the eye of the beholder.

Why is it so difficult to follow their spiritual message
To bring our hearts in tune with one another
To create a tapestry without strife?

Does the message in the garden call us
To see what we have been missing
In this multicultural life?

Dandy Lions

Those prolific golden yellow flowers
      keep sprouting up everywhere
from seeds blown or tracked,
      ensuring enough for all to share.

These age-old weeds of nefarious reputation,
      around at least since Biblical sowings
are the bane of lawncare toilers,
      in spite of their rather stunning showings.

Coveted by some for their lion-toothed greens,
      a gourmet treat in such culinary circles,
while others have forsaken the grape,
      creating a wine from these yellow miracles.

Dandy-lions are favorites with very young children
      whose endless bouquets are cause to celebrate.
So get in touch with your inner child,
      consider bouquets as they begin to populate.

Springtime Marsh Life

Teaming with animals and plant life
Whether fresh or salty waters
Springtime marshes offer ever-changing views
And abundant food for those who dwell there.

Many mysteries abound, awaiting discovery
In these rich ecosystems
With their natural pollution filters
Working in harmony to benefit all.

Behold early sightings of tadpoles
Fiddler crabs and the whitest egrets
Marsh wrens weaving nests from grasses
Oysters rhythmically filtering the waters.

Whose life has not been enriched
By views of undulating spartina grasses
Or the sudden arrival of cattails or water lilies
As well as mysterious evolutions of marsh species?

A significant life experience is lost
If one never sees such seasonal mysteries
In one of these cradles of nature
Signaling Springtime at its' best.

Queen Anne's Lace

Along roadsides and across dry fields
Her crowns of lacy umbels wave
While others curling inward
Create a bird's nest image.
When mingled with brown-eyed susans,
Red clover and goldenrod,
Despite being named invasive weeds
Create a landscape to behold.
Few see beyond her lacy veils
To the many gifts bestowed
To birds and moles who seek her shelter
And are grateful for the haven.
And though her family tree once bore
Our well known carrots and healing tonics
Her taproots offer only now
A tasty morsel for those who'd dare it.

Songs To Share

Suddenly songs everywhere, signaling Spring
With mysterious messages
Meant for one another
Of their kind or sort.

While another specie of our kind
Responds with joy on sightings
With recognition of their songs
And welcomes their return.

Whether the call of a Swainson's Warbler
Or the chirping of a Purple Martin
Their music in the air
Sets our hearts singing.

And from the time of their arrival
Our gardens seem to thrive
With their consumption of the garden pests
That would otherwise stay alive.

Their courtship rituals include their songs,
With posturing and displaying
Advertising their vigor and voracity
A rivalry aimed at reproduction.

Then at last their distinctive songs
Become their own home schooling
Teaching their young to carry on
With such joyful songs to share.

A Coat Of Many Colors

With a mind of her own
Mother Nature decides
Exactly when to peak
With her coat of many colors.

A crisp chill in the air
Trees all ablaze
Autumn's sounds and smells
Complete the transformation.

With great joy and delight
We welcome the coat
For its gift to all our senses
Unparalleled by any others.

Paddling Music

Gliding through the water
       Creating a symphony
With effortless conducting
       Engaging all the players.

Soft sounds of breezes blowing
       Across the rippling waters
Sea creatures offering vibrations and voices
       While birds overhead add melodies.

Whether seeking solitude or harmony
       Indescribable feelings await
The purposeful paddler
       Who chooses this music to celebrate.

Dolphin's Play

I wait and watch each early morn
Hoping to see the dolphins at play.
And as if on cue, a pair of fins appear
And the magical whistling begins
In rhythm as they ride the waves.

Could they possibly sense the joy they bring
Instantly leaving me breathless
As a returning pod, in pairs
Comes with a chorus of whistles and clicking
Then, without notice, all disappear.

These early morning sightings
Can surely make my day
As I have added expectations
That Flipper might be amongst them
When they all come out to play.

The Meditating Cat

Marco joined our quiet setting
         as we began our meditations
Needing very few assurances
         that this was his place, too.

He settled in as we began
         to breath and meditate
Adding his own focus on
         mindfulness and presence.

None knew his inner secret
         and he alone went there
We simply felt him as one of us
         with spiritual places to share.

News of his demise from cancer
         and his physical separation
Will leave us all deeply saddened
         without his meditations.

I know that we will think of him
         as we attempt to calm our minds
And perhaps he will join us then
         showing the patience we cannot find.

Lady Bug, Lady Bug

"Lady bug, lady bug, fly away home"
Who doesn't remember this old nursery rhyme,
The first encounter with her red and black dome
Or being repulsed by her pungent slime?

And the awe when her sheerest wings appeared
And tales of her powers to grant a wish
Were trumped by the stories
That she smelled with her feet!

The fact that her kind populated the globe
Further captured our interest and made us suspicious
What possible role in evolution
Was dangling before us and throughout the world?

Only recent revelations have helped us to see
Why she and her kin populate the earth.
Why she saves both ours and the farmers' plantings
And lets nature do what it was intended to do.

To survive and thrive in a non-toxic environment
That helps us to feed a world population
We need lady bugs, lady bugs to rid us of pests
That our flowers and crops will continue to thrive.

A Raven Or A Crow

So what is the difference, you may say
Between a Raven and a Crow?
Why should I insist on such distinction
When so few really care to know.

It has been said of our family tree
There are lots of distinguishing features
In fact, it is claimed we are at the top
As far as the avian pyramid reaches.

Others note that we are far more clever,
Intelligent, adaptable and resourceful
As far as corvids go, our voices range
On a scale with a hundred choices.

We are known to fly higher, wing to wing
With our long-term mates close-by
Performing aerial acrobatics
Or seeking former nesting locations.

And when my family tree is growing
We always provide the edibles
For the mother of the next generation
While she sits for the eggs' incubation.

So while the crow may strut about
Similar in color and occupation
We hope that you will look more closely
And lower your expectations.

The Dog Walker

Oh, you have a smiling voice
Promising a joyful romp, I think
And maybe a hug or two
Just for being me?

Please come back again real soon
For I can hardly wait
My master's naps are growing longer
And I so miss going outside the gate.

Oh, you are here again, and with treats
And another doggie, too?
I do like the smell of her
And I am getting over feeling blue.

Just hop into the car you say
But where do we plan to go?
I cannot be away too long, you see
For my master will wake and wait for me.

Game, Set!

Game, set! As spirited a call today as in years gone by
But today with less certainty on either side
Though each sets their sights with rackets held high
For a final victory smash to uphold their pride.

While visible knee braces and invisible stints
Are warning signs just across the net
It's a mirror image of the others' imprints
With odds to neither in these final sets.

Still they routinely challenge calls of "out"
Undaunted by retorts of "fading vision."
They know well the callers' fear of a rout
As well as Mother Nature's unkind decisions.

Each knows that there will be a final gauntlet
And quietly harbors with dread and fear
The time of judgment with no sign of a net
Only memories of the triumphs that once were dear.

Yard Sales

It must be the season
Those perennial front yard crops
With beauty only in the eye of the beholder
Are now sprouting up everywhere.

There's chairs and tables, jewels and junk
Books, baskets, and bathroom scales
And Aunt Jenny's wonderful wedding gifts
Still with gift tag hanging.

Tolls for different kinds of gardens
Kitchen gadgets, some like new
All offered at bargain prices
And just too good to pass them by.

Yet stopping is not in my best interest
There's already a growing crop at home
Enough to plant on my own front lawn
And lots to donate to my neighbor.

Rules, Probability, And Communication

Whether it is Rubber or Duplicate
Trick-taking is the goal of the game.
Providing endless hour of entertainment
And exercises for the brain.

Each of the points of the compass
Employ memory tactics to remain alert
And there is even a roll for a dummy
Providing players with drinks or deserts.

This ancient game of skill and chance
Rules, probability and communication
May be played in parlors or even parks
With a life-long foursome or a cast of strangers

While it is never quite the same
One may even resort to a computer game
And virtually play alone, or go on line
With all manner of willing unknowns.

That Times Columnist

She makes me smile, laugh out loud, shutter.
The most alpha of alaphas.

The most authoritative keeper
Of political Y files.

The most insightful sister
Of their X file wanna-bes.

Consummate observer of White House traffic
On extended stays or just passing through.

She tries to close the gender gap
In ways we'd never consider

While exposing the "Chimera of equality"
And how sexual politics influences elections.

Making me smile, laugh out loud, shutter
And come back for more.

An Old Treasure Chest

It's nearly too heavy to lift with ease
Though filled with treasures sure to please
Spellings, meanings, pronunciations
Usage, etymologies and related occupations.

Exquisite expressions for creating moods
As well as for describing exotic foods.
Descriptions of places, origins and seas
Symbols, sounds, states and keys.

History, dates, major ocean deeps
Waterfalls, mountains, and major peaks
Volcanoes, rivers, weights and measures
Are but a few of the special treasures

Found in the more than two thousand pages
Of my old treasure chest-
The Random House Dictionary of the English Language—
The unabridged edition.

Just Passing On

A lifetime of accumulations are closing in on me
Acquiring was fun, now please set me free!
This flotsam and jetsam clutters my life spaces
And rivals new awareness of wrinkled faces.

So, passing stuff on is my new disposition
Uncluttering surely worthy of a new life's mission.
Sure, I'll catalogue it all in the gray-matter's recesses
But my goal now is seeking some new addresses.

For the bonnets and books, baskets and jugs
Many with reminders of long-ago hugs.
Pottery and pictures, tools without needs
Will no longer be growing and spreading like weeds.

Reflecting on the reality of my own sure demise
Made this act of PASSING ON, both worthy and wise!
So, step right up, take a book, a bust, a traveler's treasure
Make an offer, take a gift, but with caution and measure.

Those Other Crustaceans

Maine's best-kept secret is out!
Those other crustaceans
From our frigid waters and robust tides
Produce happy oysters and happy eaters.

From Maine's pristine waters and estuaries
Whether straight from the water
Or as gussied-up Rockefellars
These other crustaceans will tweak your palate.

And oyster lovers need only one taste
To adopt these bounteous bivalves
To return again and again
In anticipation of generous rewards.

Just Dozing

It's where he goes
When life's puzzles
Begin to overwhelm him
With weighty worries

One eye checks
Every now and then.
Has the puzzle been resolved,
Have answers appeared?

Is dozing time up?
Or must he retreat again
To the place where images
Pass without consequences.

A Hearty Octogenarian

Oh the thoughts of becoming an octogenarian
As I race toward the finish line
Are making me joyful and jubilant
Since I have already passed my time.

I think of all the gifts and wonders
That I have been privileged to share
With generous hearts and spirits
Who have been there with so much care.

The only wish that I might make
Is to go there with some immunity
Escaping the worst of fibrous tangles
And remaining mentally nimble and witty.

The Gifts Of Aging

I hardly mind the aches or pains
Or the challenges before me
When I reflect on the joyful times
That come as gifts of aging.

For just when time seems running out
And a sense of loss arises
I meet unexpected pleasures
In the many acts of kindness.

I see new-found sights and sounds
As Mother Nature spins her magic
And brilliant creatures great and small
Providing endless entertainment.

I see ever-changing garden gifts
Once missed in the rush of everyday
Voices and faces filled with love
Unconditional, without reservation.

And now I know I might have missed
These unexpected pleasures
Nor been rewarded day after day
With these wondrous gifts of aging.

Get A Life!

Chill out, don't pout!
Find your M.O.
Give your spirit clout
Spend it like dough.

Seek others with vibes
To celebrate life
Keep adventure alive
And avoid the strife.

Be giving and grateful
Share all that you can
No gift is too small
So make a plan.

Our Yin And Yang

If I am yin
And you are yang
Can't we just get together
And make the balance right?

My yin is soft and yielding
Your yang, so hard with might
One seeing a world to contest
The other, but a place to rest.

But both, they say
Must within each dwell
For energy to flow
And make the balance right.

For a perfect blend is healing
To the spirit of a challenger
Your energy offering enough for both
My softness providing our souls with grace.

Playing With Inner Gorillas

Imagine growing up without inner gorillas.
Without peeking over gates and down dark corridors
Without seeing faces, wondering who, where, why?
Without secrets, spinning sorrows, mysteries and lies.

Imagine our beautiful dreams replacing an ugly past
Joys clouding over secret sorrows
Sunshine washing clean the script
Would the inner gorillas simply disappear?

Do others crush them into remission
Wish them underground
Bury the battered bones
Deny their existence?

Night Visitors

Quiet breaths, rising and falling
In perfect harmony
With the gliding waves
Both with a pulse and rhythm
Promising deep retreats to reassuring places.

Until nocturnal visitors
Challenged the rhythms
Bringing conflict heretofore unknown
With unrelenting stress
Upon this peaceful bosom.

Whose stories are these
Intruding upon my reverie?
What sense is there
In crushing a peaceful soul
With such hallucinations.

Then labored breaths
Awakened me
To twinkling stars and a moonlit path
Of gentle waves and assurances
That it was but a wayward dream.
With hallucinations that are unreal.

Walking In Pain

Walking in pain, listening to the rain
Wishing you were here
To soften my fear
        -of days to come.

Alone in my sorrow, with no tomorrow
Hushed, tightened breath
So abandoned and bereft

Without your love, there is none of
Your calm and reassuring grace
And I alone must face
        -of days to come

Where did we go wrong, lose our life's song
Our trips to Mars
Skies filled with stars.

Why can't we have those yesterdays
This pain I'd gladly trade
For earlier pledges made
        -of days to come.

Anger

In an instant
Boiling up
Over the top
Loss of control
Disintegration!

Disappointment, fear, pride
Unconscious revenge
What's behind it all
Why can't I let it go?

Why can't I stop
Shake my fears, swallow my pride
Take control of my emotions
Learn the devastating consequences?

Yet it has become clear
There are lasting aftermaths
For me
And for them.

It's not about love or hate
About right or wrong
It's about me
And my need to face my demons
And to begin to grow up.

Mother Nature

There were sides to her
    You would never know.
A motherless child, pained by abandonment
    So many years ago.

Her ready smile concealed
    The loss of love and identity
Made her fearful of trust,
    Yet eager to be trusted.

There were years of seeking surrogates
    Waiting for another
With unconditional love
    To take the place of a mother.

And then she discovered a miracle
    Quietly all around her
The nurturing gifts of Mother Nature
    Erasing the pain and absent mother.

New Life To Share

By Dee Dee Moore

Soft sobs filled her chest, silent tears crushing forward
Unable to hold back the pain
Despite all the wondrous love and support
The mighty floodgates opened again.

Rational thoughts were lost in the stream
Reflecting only doubts and fears
Storm drains quickly plugged with with grief
Overflowing with the quiet tears.

Mammograms, MRI's, Ultrasounds, Core Biopsies, all
Brought confirmation, resignation, pulling down the spirit
Tomorrow's courage and hope were hovering
But not yet available for her to hear it.

Then blessings came in the sentinel's clarity
In the breast's excision with precision and care
In the surgeon's confidence and assurances
Offering time and reflection on new life to share.

Coming To Grips

The verdict is in
The waves have washed up
The truth can be told
The time has come.

And yet her life surges ahead
With the many gifts left behind
And a lifetime of graces
Which have enriched so many lives.

We must not weep
This life calls forth
A celebration, rejoicing,
Commemorating vitality, beauty and love.

Reunion At Sea

As you cast my ashes out to the sea
Fear not, I will not be alone
Those who have preceded me
Have prepared my headstone.

Of Gamboling creatures
Choreographed with song
Of waves rhythmic overtures
To carry me along.

When the sun sets today on the ocean blue
Treasure our love but
As the sun rises tomorrow, begin anew
Bring all of your energy to life.

I will be there for you
With a fresh breeze and song
I will watch your new beginnings
As you paddle along.

Oh, They're From Away

Are we really just "from away"
  Or do we actually nest
For longer than a mating season
  Or just for time to rest?

Do we follow the season's endings
  Or arrive in time to greet the new
Do we bring our own songs with us
  Or string along with local coo?

Do we embrace the many welcome mats
  Or feel a bit of teetering
When friends offer us open arms
  And share their lives' meterings?

Will we ever settle down at journey's end
  And bring our own joyful songs
Or will we continue to migrate mentally
  And just pretend that we belong?

Coming Of Age

Wasn't it only yesterday
When your capes and quips amazed us all
While brandishing sticks and swords
With stories grand and tall.

Wasn't it only yesterday
That your disappearing acts
Caused angst and fear in all of us
When you seemed to slip between the cracks.

I know it was at an early age, able to parlez francais
That you inspired and wowed us all
And that your drama pitches got attention
As they should have for one so small.

Then Harry Potter came into being
And inspired our culinary capers
To my delight, you chose birthday "dirt"
For your age-appropriate tapers.

A work in progress cannot be denied
Your new voice speaks with growing pride
Of personal commitment
And your fulfillment of goals.

And now, here you are before us
And before this congregation
A special rite of passage
A Coming of Age Celebration.

The Gift Of A Lily

No ordinary lily
Could ever fill my garden
With such delight
Nor enrich my life
As the essence of her spirit.

With her joyful arrival
The universe bloomed anew
As she approached her new surroundings
Brought questions to explore
Offered new perspectives for me to see.

Annual summer visits, full of creative promise
Brought spontaneous dances on wisps of wind
Fairy houses made with an architect's eye
Sewing, knitting and paddling adventures
Then costumes and masks at the Opera House
All with a spirit of diligence and sharing.

Now about to fully blossom
More than a namesake from pages or stages
Her journey is destined
To enrich many more lives
With Life's unexpected pleasures.

And like other lilies around the world
Whether alpine, prairie,
Or meadow species,
She will delight each beholder
With a spirit of anticipation.

And Lily or Lillian, whichever she chooses
For the many faces
About to bloom
Will always bring joy and delight
Into her Mimi's room.

Edible Pursuits

A late springtime ritual has begun
     the hunt for the illusive fungi,
particularly after the April showers
     when mysterious fruits begin to arise.

Good fortune can offer a variety of caps
     bell-shaped, conical or convex
inviting both speculation and temptation
     with maturing fruits to index.

Then behold, a find of the choicest edibles.
     a patch of delectable chanterelles
as yet undiscovered by any others,
     including the four-legged fanciers.

Still further into the decaying oak woods
     where chance explodes with colors
the hunt reveals the rose-red bolete,
     a choicest edible among all others.

Among the skeptics, there will be those
     who might question this pursuit.
Though seeking edible fungi from forest floors,
     Is a worthy challenge for which to root.

Syllabub For Syllables

Syllabub solid, or separated
Can nourish the mind of a poet
And while cookies or cake
Can serve as rewards
This British invention can sow it!

A cold lemony sweet
Served up in soft peaks or
Separated from tart whey beneath
Whichever you choose will surely delight
And syllabub for syllables rise to a new heights.

Ode To Parsnips

By Dee Dee Moore

Oh those garden treasures
Will soon be on my plate
Sure, a frost would enhance their flavor
But I simply cannot wait.

And I'll later double my pleasure
When winter chills abound
I'll dig them up through the snow
And pass them all around.

For a rich and nutty flavor
Bringing gourmet to any dish
Whether simply pureed or sautéed
In a soup, a salad or a pudding wish.

Poetry: My Mojo

A poet, you may say
But not a laureate.
A journal keeper rather
Connecting the dots, or not.

Observer of Rituals and dances
That Mother Nature provides
String them along in song
Creating simple verses.

Sometimes lofty observations
Woven into stories
Filled with deep emotions
From meaningful events past.

Poetry, as creative expression
Whether in rhyme, or meter, or neither
Provides a personal journal
And a gift to share with others.

A Poet's Preoccupation

How many cold cups of coffee
Have awaited the poet's quest
For just the right mood or memory
To be translated into verse?

How true must the meters measure
To convey the sights and sounds
For expressing the real intention
Of poetic praise or recognition?

Then early mornings grow longer
Beyond the time intended
As words beg for alteration
And finally, satisfied and savored.

Real Writing

Whatever was I thinking
When first I hit on you
Was it the old familiar keyboard
Of Smith Corona days?

While at first somewhat comforting
You soon left me in a daze
Your settings all seemed fickle
And at best left me crazed.

Getting the words on paper
Did not happened as I wrote
And communing with the printer
Another mystery unresolved.

Then just when I thought I had it
And became a bit more patient
You quickly took away my work
And left me defenseless.

Now having used up all my patience
Leaving few creative juices
I have decided to return
To real writing with my Ticonderoga.

Appeal To The Candidates

I listen, watch and weigh
The words that fill the air
For a voice close to my own
With concerns for world peace,
Truth, a valued treasure
Hunger, a concept unknown
Partisanship, of little measure.

Instead I hear words of strife,
Accusation, blame, hollow words,
Brazen navigation of the truth,
Juxtaposing the charges of
Keep the campaign clean
But win at all costs.

The mindless pundits adds their cause
Fueled by demanded ratings
And in the end, we all retreat
Remembering only the Hope for
Cooperation and collaboration
And man's humanity for all mankind.

From Here To There

Where will this journey take me
With no schedule or prescribed destination?
How will I know when I have arrived
Whether the message matters at all?

What joy is there in going there
With little known conclusion
If not the delight and discovery
Of an awareness not before known.

About the Author

Dee Dee Moore is a Professor Emeritus and former Dean of College of Education and Human Development at the University of Southern Maine. A passionate teacher as well as a mediator in Maine Courts for more than twenty years, has fueled her observations of Human Nature, and given voice to another passion, poetry. Since her retirement, Dee Dee has enjoyed writing children's books and poetry, having published a children's book about her mischievous golden retriever and more than fifty poems. While most of her subjects come from observations of Maine mornings in her beloved Deer Isle, Maine, her years in Hilton Head Island, have provided another of her favorite settings for observing Mother Nature at work.

She is the mother of two delightful daughters and two exceptional grandchildren.